Usain Bolt

By Jeff Savage

AMAZING ATHLETES

Lerner Publications Company • Minneapolis

Copyright © 2013 by Lerner Publishing Group, Inc.

All rights reserved. International copyright secured. No part of this book may be reproduced, stored in a retrieval system, or transmitted in any form or by any means—electronic, mechanical, photocopying, recording, or otherwise—without the prior written permission of Lerner Publishing Group, Inc., except for the inclusion of brief quotations in an acknowledged review.

Lerner Publications Company
A division of Lerner Publishing Group, Inc.
241 First Avenue North
Minneapolis, MN 55401 U.S.A.

Website address: www.lernerbooks.com

Library of Congress Cataloging-in-Publication Data

Savage, Jeff, 1961–
    Usain Bolt / by Jeff Savage.
        p.   cm. — (Amazing athletes)
    Includes index.
    ISBN 978–1–4677–1088–6 (lib. bdg. : alk. paper)
    1. Bolt, Usain, 1986—Juvenile literature. 2. Runners (Sports)—Jamaica—Biography—Juvenile literature. I. Title.
GV1061.15.B66S38 2013
796.42092—dc23 [B]   2012032474

Manufactured in the United States of America
1 – MG – 12/31/12

TABLE OF CONTENTS

Olympic Legend	4
A Fast Start	8
Comfortable at Home	12
Lightning Bolt	18
World's Fastest Human	23
Selected Career Highlights	29
Glossary	30
Further Reading & Websites	31
Index	32

The 100-meter finalists burst from the starting blocks at the 2012 Olympic Games. Usain is third from the left.

OLYMPIC LEGEND

Usain Bolt blazed down the track. He was racing with the world's fastest runners at the 2012 Olympic Games. The crowd of 80,000 in London, England, roared louder at each step.

At the halfway point of this 100-meter final, Usain was in sixth place. Justin Gatlin from the United States was in front. Yohan Blake, Usain's Jamaican countryman, was second. With mere seconds to go, Usain made a sudden burst. He moved into fifth place . . . then third . . . then second . . . Usain took the lead!

Usain *(left)* races past other runners in the 100-meter final.

Usain was already famous. At the Olympic Games four years earlier, he had won three gold medals—in the 100-meter, 200-meter, and 4 x 100-meter relay—all in world-record times. No runner in track history had ever done that.

Cheeks puffing, arms pumping, Usain stretched across the finish line in 9.63 seconds. He broke his own Olympic record!

Usain celebrated by high-fiving fans along the front row. He did his Lightning Bolt pose. "He's a showman," said Gatlin, "and he puts on a great show."

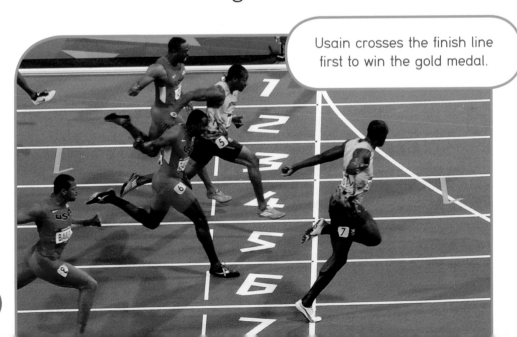

Usain crosses the finish line first to win the gold medal.

Usain celebrates with some of his fans.

Four days later, Usain was back on the track for the 200-meter race. At the start, he was off in a dash. He swept around the curve, moving farther out front with every long **stride**. Gritting his teeth, he got so far ahead that he had time to slow down the last few steps. He put his finger to his mouth, as if to quiet his critics. Usain explained, "A lot of people doubted me. I was just telling them, 'You can stop talking now because I am a legend.'"

7

Jennifer Bolt, Usain's mother, stands in front of the family home in Sherwood Content in 2009.

A Fast Start

Usain St. Leo Bolt was born August 21, 1986, to Wellesley and Jennifer Bolt. Usain lives on the island of Jamaica in the Caribbean Sea. He was raised with his brother, Sadiki, and his sister, Sherine. The family lived in a small wooden house in the village of Sherwood

Content. Wellesley worked in a shop selling meat, eggs, and milk. Jennifer picked fruit in the nearby fields.

Usain was born with a condition called scoliosis. His spine curved more than normal. It hurt for him to sit or lie in the same position for long. Other children liked to sit still and play with marbles. But Usain wasn't comfortable shooting marbles. He preferred action sports. He often played soccer and **cricket** with his brother in front of his house. "When I was young," Usain said, "I didn't really think about anything other than sports."

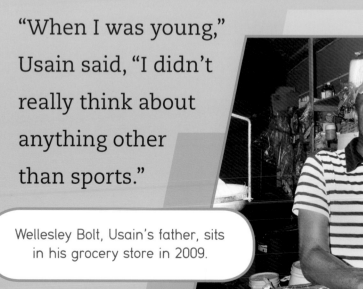

Wellesley Bolt, Usain's father, sits in his grocery store in 2009.

9

When Usain was nine, his family was concerned that he was too focused on sports. Usain's father took his son to a doctor. But the doctor didn't believe anything was wrong with Usain's love of sports. Soon afterward, the boy started running. At the age of 10, he joined his school track-and-field team. Two years later, he was the fastest runner at Waldensia Primary School. But Usain's favorite sport was cricket. "I was a good **fast bowler**," he said. But his cricket coach at William Knibb Memorial High School urged Usain to focus on track and field.

Usain won his first high school medal in the 80-meter **hurdles**. He finished third and took

Usain gives back to his home country through the Usain Bolt Foundation. The group gives money and time to help children, hospitals, and others in need.

Usain attended and ran track for William Knibb Memorial High School in Trelawny, Jamaica.

home a bronze medal. In his next **meet**, he finished in second place for a silver medal in the 200-meter race. Usain got to travel to the nearby island of Barbados for the 2001 Caribbean Free Trade Association (CARIFTA) Games. He won silver medals in the 200- and 400-meter races.

Usain runs the 200-meter race at the 2002 World Junior Championships.

COMFORTABLE AT HOME

One month before Usain's 16th birthday, he competed in the 2002 World Junior Championships. Athletes from around the world came to Kingston, the capital of Jamaica. Usain was proud to wear the black, green, and gold colors of his nation.

The biggest crowd in World Junior Championship history packed the stands. They roared with delight when Usain won Jamaica's only gold medal. He blazed first to the finish line in the 200-meter race. He had become the youngest junior world champion in history!

Usain stood 6 feet, 5 inches tall. He towered over other runners. His long legs allowed him to take longer strides. In 2004, he broke the junior world record in the 200-meter race with a stunning time of 19.93 seconds.

Usain takes longer strides than most runners. A longer stride usually takes more time. Not for Usain. He takes as many strides as most other runners.

Usain was offered **scholarships** from top colleges in the United States. The schools wanted Usain to run on their track-and-field teams. He turned them down. "I can't live outside Jamaica," he said. "This is where I'm comfortable." Usain practiced on a worn track that once was a sugarcane field. He used old training equipment. He did not mind.

Usain had focused on the 200-meter event for two years. He begged Coach Mills to let him compete in the 100-meter race. Early in 2008, Usain stunned the track world at a meet in Jamaica by running 100 meters in 9.76 seconds. It was the second-fastest time in history. Then he broke the world record at a meet in New York City with a time of 9.72 seconds. "We look like junior high kids out there compared to [Usain]," said runner Darvis Patton.

Usain *(center)* sets a new world record in the 100-meter race in New York in 2008.

Two months later, Usain traveled to Beijing, China, for the 2008 Olympics. He was determined to do better in his second Olympic Games.

Usain *(right)* moves ahead of the other runners in the 100-meter final at the 2008 Olympic Games.

LIGHTNING BOLT

Usain's mother traveled with him to Beijing. His father stayed home, afraid to fly on an airplane. Two days before the 100-meter event, Usain spoke with his father on the telephone. "Don't worry, Dad," Usain said. "I'm going to win this race for you."

18

In the men's 100-meter final, Usain sprang from the starting blocks with the rest of the runners. He immediately took the lead. With each stride, he stretched his lead more. He was well out in front after a few seconds.

With about 30 meters to go, Usain turned his head to see if anyone was close. They were not. He swept his arms back like airplane wings. He thumped his chest once before he crossed the line. He finished in 9.69 seconds, crushing the world and Olympic records.

Usain celebrates his new world-record time in the 100-meter race.

Runners go as fast as they can during the 100-meter race. The distance is short, so they don't have to save their energy for the end. The winner of the 100-meter event at the Olympic Games is considered the fastest runner in the world.

"He's a freak of nature," said Donovan Bailey, once a world record holder in the 100-meter race. "Usain is amazing, absolutely amazing." To celebrate, Usain stood like an archer. He cocked one arm back and aimed the other at the sky like an arrow. This became known as the Lightning Bolt pose. Back in Jamaica, people filled the streets waving flags and

Usain and some partners opened a restaurant and sports bar in Kingston called Tracks and Records. The restaurant's logo shows Usain striking the Lightning Bolt pose.

beating drums. Music blared through the night.

The 200-meter race was three days later. What did Usain do while he waited? "All I did was relax," he said. "I ate my nuggets at McDonald's. I chilled, I focused." In the race, Usain ran for gold again. He crossed the finish line in 19.30 seconds to set world and Olympic records.

Usain celebrated with a dance. The "Happy Birthday" song played over the stadium's loudspeakers. Usain's 22nd birthday was the next day.

Usain celebrates his 200-meter win by doing the Lightning Bolt pose.

Two days later, Usain teamed with three Jamaican runners to win the 4 x 100-meter relay in world-record time. Usain had become the first sprinter in Olympic history to win gold medals in all three events.

Usain returned to Jamaica a national hero! A parade was held in his honor in Kingston. He went to the United States, where he appeared on television talk shows. He starred in commercials for airplanes and credit cards. Usain had become a global star.

Usain *(right)* hands the baton to teammate Asafa Powell during the 4 x 100-meter relay.

Usain sets a new world record of 9.58 seconds in the 100-meter final at the World Championships in 2009.

WORLD'S FASTEST HUMAN

At the 2009 World Championships in Berlin, Germany, Usain set new world records in the 100- and 200-meter races. "With Bolt in the race, we already know who is going to win," said former gold-medal runner Michael Johnson.

Usain began to relax too much. He stopped training hard. His coach grew concerned. "He has done more in his short career than most people have done in a lifetime," said Coach Mills. "It is important that he doesn't become too satisfied with what he has achieved."

At the 2011 World Championships in Daegu, South Korea, Usain was eliminated from a race for a **false start**.

In 2010, sports drink company Gatorade released a new flavor in Usain's honor. The drink is called Bolt Lemon Ice.

Usain *(right)* plays cricket in 2009.

Usain poses with a book he wrote about his life in 2010.

At the 2012 Olympic trials in Jamaica, he lost the 100- and 200-meter races to fellow Jamaican Yohan Blake. But Usain still made the Olympic team.

Was Usain no longer the world's fastest human? The Olympic Games in London, England, were one month away. "I have to show the world I'm the best," said Usain. "I can come back. It's not like I was blown away. Now I know what I need to do to get it right."

At the Olympics, Usain blazed to three gold medals. His timing was perfect. Usain's country had gained its independence from the United Kingdom 50 years earlier. "I wanted to

Usain *(top left)* and his teammates celebrate setting a world record in the 4 x 100-meter relay. This was Usain's third gold medal at the 2012 Olympic Games.

give Jamaica a great birthday present," Usain said. "I wanted to show the world that I'm still Number 1, I'm still the best."

At the medal ceremony for the 200-meter event, Usain leaped to the top step of the podium. He kissed his gold medal.

Usain celebrates his gold medal win in the 200-meter event.

Usain has enjoyed many things by being the fastest human in the world. He has earned millions of dollars. He has spent time with his favorite soccer team, Manchester United of England. He has given running tips to soccer superstar Cristiano Ronaldo.

Usain enjoys his good fortune. But he knows that hard work and winning on the track are his tickets to glory. "I've said it over the years, that when it comes to championships, this is what I do."

Usain *(left, in hat)* takes part in a fun run to raise money for a children's hospital in Jamaica in 2012.

Selected Career Highlights

2012 Won gold medal in 100-meter race at Olympic Games
Won gold medal in 200-meter race at Olympic Games
Won gold medal in 4 x 100-meter relay at Olympic Games

2011 Won gold medal in 200-meter race at World Championships
Won gold medal in 4 x 100-meter relay at World Championships

2010 Won 200-meter race at Jamaica International Invitational with a time of 19.56 seconds, the fourth-fastest ever

2009 Won gold medal in 100-meter race at World Championships
Set world record time in 100-meter race at 9.58 seconds
Won gold medal in 200-meter race at World Championships
Set world record time in 200-meter race at 19.19 seconds
Won gold medal in 4 x 100-meter relay at World Championships

2008 Won gold medal in 100-meter race at Olympic Games
Set world and Olympic record times in 100-meter race at 9.69 seconds
Won gold medal in 200-meter race at Olympic Games
Set world and Olympic record times in 200-meter race at 19.30 seconds
Won gold medal in 4 x 100-meter relay at Olympic Games
Set world and Olympic record times in 4 x 100-meter relay at 37.10 seconds

2007 Won silver medal in 200-meter race at World Championships
Won silver medal in 4 x 100-meter relay at World Championships

2006 Won silver medal in 200-meter race at World Cup

2005 Won gold medal in 200-meter race at Central American and Caribbean Championships

2004 Won gold medal in 200-meter race, 4 x 100-meter relay, and 4 x 400-meter relay at CARIFTA Games

Glossary

coordination: the ability to maintain balance and rhythm between arms, legs, and other parts of a body in motion

core muscles: a group of muscles that connect the upper and lower body and support the spine. These include abdominals (abs) as well as muscles in the hips and lower back.

cricket: a bat-and-ball sport similar to baseball played between two teams of 11 players each

false start: leaving the starting blocks before the starting gun is fired to start the race

fast bowler: the person who throws the cricket ball with great speed to get out a batter

hurdles: a race in which runners jump over barriers

meet: an event at which a number of track-and-field contests are held

scholarships: money from colleges to help pay for a student's expenses such as housing, tuition, and books

stride: a step taken while running

Further Reading & Websites

Cantor, George. *Usain Bolt*. Detroit: Lucent Books, 2011.

Frederick, Shane. *Track & Field*. Mankato, MN: Creative Education, 2012.

Gifford, Clive. *The Inside Story of Track and Field*. New York: Rosen Central, 2012.

Sutcliffe, Jane. *Jesse Owens*. Minneapolis: Millbrook Press, 2001.

International Association of Athletics Federations
http://www.iaaf.org
The official website of the world governing body for track and field features event results, late-breaking news, biographies of hundreds of athletes, information on school and youth programs, and much more.

Sports Illustrated Kids
http://www.sikids.com
The *Sports Illustrated Kids* website covers all sports, including track and field.

Usain Bolt: The Official Site
http://www.usainbolt.com
Usain's official site features a biography, photos, a song list of Usain's favorite music, information on his foundation, and a sign-up link for his fan club.

Index

4 x 100-meter relay, 6, 22, 26
100-meter race, 5, 6, 16, 18–20, 23, 25
200-meter race, 6, 7, 11, 13, 14, 21, 23, 25, 27

Blake, Yohan, 5, 25
Bolt, Jennifer, 8–9, 18
Bolt, Sadiki, 8–9
Bolt, Sherine, 8
Bolt, Usain: criticism of, 14; early life of, 8–11; endorsements by, 22, 24; health of, 9, 15; height of, 13; and sports, 9–10; stride of, 13; world records by, 6–9, 13, 16, 19–23, 26
Bolt, Wellesley, 8–10, 18

coordination, 15
core muscles, 15

Gatlin, Justin, 5, 6

Jamaica, 8, 13–14, 16, 20–21, 22, 25, 26–27

Lightning Bolt pose, 6–7, 20

Mills, Glen, 15–16, 24

Olympic Games: 2004, 14; 2008, 6, 17–22; 2012, 4–7, 25–28

scoliosis, 9

Tracks and Records, 20

Usain Bolt Foundation, 10

World Championships: 2002 Junior, 12–13; 2009, 23; 2011, 24

Photo Acknowledgments

The images in this book are used with the permission of: © Harry E. Walker/MCT via Getty Images, p. 4; © Phil Walter/Getty Images, p. 5; © Emmanuel Dunand/AFP/Getty Images, p. 6; © Adam Pretty/Getty Images, p. 7; © Ian Walton/Getty Images, pp. 8, 9, 11; © Andy Lyons/Getty Images, p. 12; © Daniel Garcia/AFP/Getty Images, p. 14; © Michael Steele/Getty Images, p. 15; AP Photo/Bill Kostroun, p. 17; Sipa via AP Images, p. 18; AP Photo/David J. Phillip, p. 19; © Carl De Souza/AFP/Getty Images, p. 21; © Jewel Samad/AFP/Getty Images, p. 22; AP Photo/Markus Schreiber, p. 23; AP Photo/Collin Reid, p. 24; AP Photo/Akira Suemori, p. 25; © Stu Forster/Getty Images, p. 26; © Franck Fife/AFP/Getty Images, p. 27; © Splash News/CORBIS, p. 28; © Mark Ralston/AFP/Getty Images, p. 29.

Front cover: © David Eulitt/Kansas City Star/MCT via Getty Images.

Main body text set in Caecilia LT Std 55 Roman 16/28.
Typeface provided by Adobe Systems.

DATE DUE

DEC 13 2018